PUTTING THE PLANET FIRST

WHAT ARE ECO-CITIES?

NANCY DICKMANN

CRABTREE
PUBLISHING COMPANY
WWW.CRABTREEBOOKS.COM

CRABTREE
PUBLISHING COMPANY
WWW.CRABTREEBOOKS.COM

Published in Canada
Crabtree Publishing
616 Welland Avenue
St. Catharines, ON
L2M 5V6

Published in the United States
Crabtree Publishing
PMB 59051
350 Fifth Ave, 59th Floor
New York, NY 10118

Published in 2019 by Crabtree Publishing Company

Printed in the USA/082018/CG20180601

Author: Nancy Dickmann

Editorial director: Kathy Middleton

Editors: Paul Mason, Elizabeth Brent, Ellen Rodger

Proofreader: Lorna Notsch

Interior design: Peter Clayman

Prepress technician: Ken Wright

Print coordinator: Katherine Berti

Images:
Cover: yyama / Shutterstock.com
All images courtesy of Shutterstock except p5: TonyV3112/
Shutterstock.com; p6–7: Joseph Sohm/Shutterstock.com; p9: kah loong
lee/Shutterstock.com; p12: Susan Montgomery/Shutterstock.com; p15:
TK Kurikawa/Shutterstock.com; p17: Igor Plotnikov/Shutterstock.com;
p21: Getty Images/Boston Globe; p23: Gallo Images – Neil Overy.

Every attempt has been made to clear copyright. Should there be any
inadvertent omission, please apply to the publisher for rectification.

The website addresses (URLs) included in this book were valid at
the time of going to press. However, it is possible that contents or
addresses may have changed since the publication of this book. No
responsibility for any such changes can be accepted by either the
author or the Publisher.

Library and Archives Canada Cataloguing in Publication

Dickmann, Nancy, author
        What are eco-cities? / Nancy Dickmann.

(Putting the planet first)
Includes index.
Issued in print and electronic formats.
ISBN 978-0-7787-5033-8 (hardcover).--
ISBN 978-0-7787-5037-6 (softcover).--
ISBN 978-1-4271-2146-2 (HTML)

        1. Urban ecology (Sociology)--Juvenile literature. 2. Sustainable urban
development--Juvenile literature. 3. City planning--Environmental aspects--
Juvenile literature. I. Title.

HT241.D53 2018   j307.76   C2018-902467-4
                                                    C2018-902468-2

Library of Congress Cataloging-in-Publication Data

Names: Dickmann, Nancy, author.
Title: What are eco-cities? / Nancy Dickmann.
Description: New York : Crabtree Publishing Company, [2019] |
    Series: Putting the planet first | Includes index.
Identifiers: LCCN 2018021423 (print) | LCCN 2018022880 (ebook) |
    ISBN 9781427121462 (Electronic) |
    ISBN 9780778750338 (hardcover) |
    ISBN 9780778750376 (pbk.)
Subjects: LCSH: Urban ecology (Sociology)--Juvenile literature. |
    Environmentalism--Juvenile literature. |
    Sustainable urban development--Juvenile literature.
Classification: LCC HT241 (ebook) | LCC HT241 .D54 2019 (print) |
    DDC 307.1/416--dc23
LC record available at https://lccn.loc.gov/2018021423

CONTENTS

WHAT IS AN ECO-CITY?

Do you live in a town or a city? Today, more than half of us do. One day soon, many city dwellers may be living in a new type of city: an eco-city.

The idea of an eco-city is that the people living there have a good quality of life, while using as few **natural resources** as possible. These natural resources include food, water, energy, and building materials.

Some older cities are making changes to become eco-cities. There are also some new cities that are being built from scratch as eco-cities.

People drive less in eco-cities, which helps the planet.

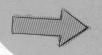

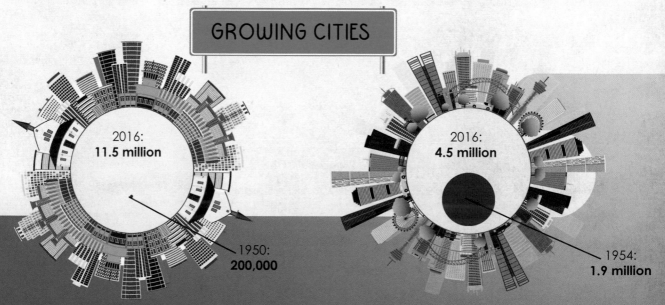

GROWING CITIES

2016:
11.5 million

1950:
200,000

Kinshasa, Democratic Republic of the Congo

2016:
4.5 million

1954:
1.9 million

Sydney, Australia

As the populations of cities grow, they use more resources.

HELPING THE PLANET

The world's population is growing, which is using up the planet's natural resources. If we use all the resources now, there will be none left for people in the future.

Eco-cities are designed to encourage people to drive their cars less and use less energy to heat and power their homes. These are ways of making urban life less harmful to the planet.

ECO-CITIES AND ECOSYSTEMS

The idea of an eco-city is based on a natural ecosystem. An ecosystem is a group of living things and the place where they live.

The parts of an ecosystem are connected. For example, some plants in an ecosystem grow in soil. Animals eat these plants to live. When the animals die, **bacteria** and insects break them down. The animals then become part of the soil.

ECOSYSTEM CITIES

In a similar way to an ecosystem, all the parts of an eco-city are designed to work together. This includes transport, housing, parks, and sewers. Resources within an eco-city provide its people with energy and food, rather than bringing these in from outside. The city's products can be reused, **recycled**, or burned to create energy.

Features that make a city more eco-friendly:

compact
housing

public
transport

green
spaces

cycle
paths

renewable
energy

waste
recycling

BIOSPHERE 2

In 1991, a group of eight scientists in Arizona started an incredible experiment. They wanted to learn how to live in harmony within an ecosystem, in a similar way to residents of eco-cities.

For two years, the scientists went to live in a complex of glass buildings—an extreme version of an eco-city. The buildings, called Biosphere 2, were designed to re-create some of Earth's natural ecosystems, such as deserts, grasslands, and tropical rain forests. Once inside, the scientists had no access to the outside world. They had to grow all their own food and generate their own power.

Research such as that done in Biosphere 2 informs the design of eco-cities.

ZERO-CARBON LIVING

One of the challenges facing eco-cities is to produce less of a gas called carbon dioxide **(CO_2). Too much carbon dioxide damages the environment.**

THE PROBLEM WITH CO_2

Carbon dioxide is released when we burn **fossil fuels** such as oil, coal, or natural gas. It builds up in the **atmosphere**, where it traps heat. This is causing Earth's average temperature to rise. The result is **climate change**, with droughts and more extreme weather conditions.

Many eco-cities want to be zero-carbon cities. This means releasing no CO_2 into the air. That's easier said than done! Most of our energy comes from fossil fuels. Everything, from driving a car to charging a phone, releases CO_2.

CO_2 EMISSIONS PER HOUSEHOLD

Sweden
**2.66 tons
(2.42 tonnes)**

China
**4.18 tons
(3.8 tonnes)**

Australia
**5.99 tons
(5.44 tonnes)**

Some countries are better than others at reducing CO_2 **emissions**.

Petaling Jaya's population is growing, but the city is still determined to cut its total carbon emissions.

PETALING JAYA

There are currently no large cities that are truly zero-carbon, but many cities are working to reduce their carbon levels as much as possible.

The city of Petaling Jaya, in Malaysia, has made a plan to help reduce its CO_2 emissions by 30 percent by the year 2030.

The plan includes using less electricity in homes and businesses and installing cleaner ways of generating energy, such as **solar panels** on buildings (see pages 10 and 11). The city will also improve its public transportation system, so that more people travel on buses instead of driving their cars. Charging stations will be installed for electric cars.

GOING RENEWABLE

To avoid burning fossil fuels, which releases CO$_2$, eco-cities use other sources of renewable energy.

Renewable energy comes from sources that will never run out, such as the Sun, wind, or running water. These types of power produce very little CO$_2$. They cause far less harm to the environment than fossil fuels do.

Sometimes, renewable energy can be generated within the eco-city itself. Examples include solar panels on buildings or **wind turbines**. Other times, an eco-city can get electricity from a solar power station in the countryside, or from an offshore wind farm.

ECO-CITY ENERGY

Solar **thermal** power provides heat

City produces sewage and wastewater, and their heat is captured and reused

Wind power provides electricity

Solar panels on homes and offices provide electricity

Power plants provide both electricity and heat

Water from oceans, rivers, and lakes provides natural cooling

City produces garbage, which is burned to generate heat

These are just some of the renewable energy sources that can power an eco-city.

One day soon, most new buildings will have solar panels built into their walls.

THE SOLAR WALL

Many people have installed solar panels on their roofs. But some architects are going one step further by making solar panels part of the buildings themselves. They replace materials normally used for roofs, skylights, or wall coverings with panels that can generate electricity.

In South Korea, one new office building has been built with a wall made of solar panels. They are special panels that shade the building's inside to keep it cool, but also let in daylight. At the same time, they generate about 10 percent of the building's electricity.

URBAN DESIGN

No city can be zero-carbon if it still has thousands of cars on the roads. This is because most cars run on gas or diesel fuel, which release CO_2 into the air.

In many cities, stores and offices are located in the center. People travel in from the edge of the city to work or go shopping. Others travel from one part of the city to another to go to school or work. If everyone makes these journeys by car, a lot of pollution is released.

New eco-cities are laid out so that people can get from place to place without using a car. Homes, stores, schools, and offices are grouped close enough together that most residents can travel by walking or cycling.

In London, England, more than 610,000 bike journeys are made each day.

TRAVELING TO WORK

Car 72%

In the U.K., most people travel to work by car.

Train 11%

Bus 5%

Bicycle 3%

Walking 4%

Other 5%

LONDON: BIKE CITY

The local government in London, England, wants more people to travel by bicycle. It has introduced two important plans to encourage people to bike.

First, London is building a network of cycle superhighways that run from the edges of the city into the center. These routes often follow main roads, but they are separate cycle paths. This will hopefully encourage more people to cycle as they will feel safer on the road.

London also has a bike-hire plan. For a small fee, people can take a bicycle at one docking station and return it to any other docking station once they have finished. There are over 10,000 bicycles available and more than 700 docking stations.

PUBLIC TRANSPORT

In bigger cities, some trips are too long to walk or cycle. If people drive cars for these journeys, it uses up fuel and releases CO$_2$. This is where public transportion comes in.

Buses, trains, and electric streetcars all help people get where they need to go. When buses and streetcars have special lanes to cut through the traffic, they are also much faster than a car.

A bus or a train does use more fuel than a car, but it can carry many more passengers. This means a full bus or train uses far less fuel per person than a car. And many cities are upgrading their bus fleets, with buses that get some or all of their power from environmentally friendly sources.

CAR VERSUS STREETCAR

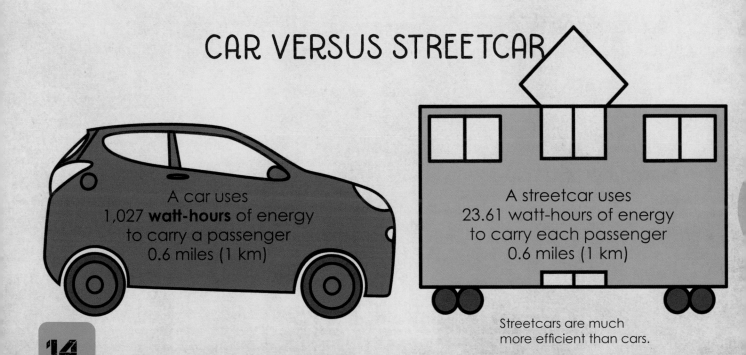

A car uses 1,027 **watt-hours** of energy to carry a passenger 0.6 miles (1 km)

A streetcar uses 23.61 watt-hours of energy to carry each passenger 0.6 miles (1 km)

Streetcars are much more efficient than cars.

Streetcar in Melbourne, Australia

TRAM-TASTIC MELBOURNE!

The city of Melbourne, in Australia, has the world's biggest streetcar network. Each year, more than 175 million streetcar journeys are made.

Streetcars are like trains, but they run on tracks along city streets instead of separate train lines. The streetcars in Melbourne are electric. The power comes from wires that run above the streetcar routes.

Melbourne is encouraging more people to use the streetcars, rather than traveling by car, by making some routes free. The streetcar system has more than 1,760 stops across the city, so traveling by streetcar is quick and easy.

ECO-HOUSING

To make getting around easier, eco-cities have to be compact. This means that people live in apartment buildings instead of single-family homes.

USING LESS ENERGY

Because apartments are usually smaller than houses, it takes less energy to heat and cool them. They also share walls, so once the whole building is warm or cool, less energy is needed to keep it at that temperature.

Homes in eco-cities are built with plenty of **insulation**, so they stay cool in summer and warm in winter. Some eco-homes make use of recycled or renewable building materials. These include straw bales, insulating foam made from seaweed, and even plastic "wood" that is actually made from recycled shopping bags!

HOUSE SIZES

Average house sizes are very different from country to county. Bigger homes typically use more energy than smaller ones.

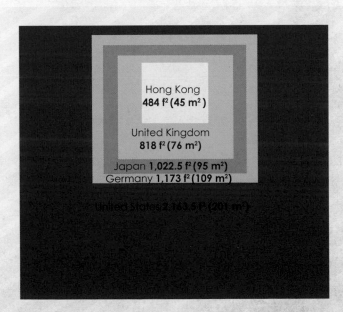

Hong Kong
484 f² (45 m²)

United Kingdom
818 f² (76 m²)

Japan **1,022.5 f² (95 m²)**
Germany **1,173 f² (109 m²)**

United States **2,163.5 f² (201 m²)**

RECYCLED HOMES

In some places, people are recycling metal shipping containers and turning them into homes. The containers can be stacked on top of each other to make apartment blocks. They are compact and affordable, and don't use much energy. Reusing existing structures in this way saves natural resources.

In France, for example, shipping containers have been converted and stacked to make housing for university students. Each container has a bathroom, living area, and small kitchen. The containers have been arranged to leave space for walkways and balconies.

These shipping containers in France provide compact, efficient homes for students.

PUBLIC BUILDINGS

A building's carbon footprint **refers to the total amount of CO_2 and other harmful gases it releases. Big buildings can have big carbon footprints.**

Making large buildings more energy efficient can help a city reduce the total amount of CO_2 it releases. As a result, many cities have passed laws that require new buildings to be energy efficient.

In France, for example, the government has made it unlawful for shops and office buildings to leave their lights on all night. Experts think this should save enough electricity to power 750,000 homes for a year.

POWERING BIG BUILDINGS

The type of energy used to power a building has a big effect on the amount of CO_2 it releases.

Using wind energy releases almost no CO_2.

Using natural gas releases 19 times as much CO_2 as wind energy.

Using coal releases 34 times as much CO_2 as wind energy.

From the top of the Reichstag's dome, visitors see an amazing view of Berlin, Germany.

GREEN PARLIAMENT

The Reichstag is a historic building in Berlin, Germany, that dates back to 1894. It is where the country's parliament meets. In 1999, the Reichstag reopened after renovations to make it more efficient. It now produces more energy than it uses.

A glass dome in the roof lets in natural light and heat, and it can be opened for ventilation. The dome has a Sun shield that tracks the Sun and blocks direct sunlight, to keep the building from getting too hot. Extra heat is used to warm fluid, which is then stored deep underground and used for heating in the winter.

WASTE MANAGEMENT

Everything we no longer need—from an empty chip bag or a pair of too-small jeans, to the grass clippings from your lawn—has to go somewhere.

LANDFILL PROBLEMS

In many cities, this garbage gets collected and buried in **landfills**. But these take up valuable space, and there is so much waste, that finding places to put it is becoming a big problem. Also, as the waste decomposes, it releases greenhouse gases, which damage the environment.

REUSE AND RECYCLING

In an eco-city, waste is reused or recycled as much as possible. Cardboard boxes and aluminum cans can be recycled into new products. Garden and food waste can be **composted** to make fertilizer. Some waste can be burned in power plants to generate electricity.

CUTTING DOWN ON GARBAGE

Between 1998 and 2015, the city of Freiburg, Germany, cut its non-recyclable waste by 85 percent.

1998
154,000 tons (140,000 metric tons) of garbage

2015
22,733 tons (20,623 metric tons) of garbage

This display at a Vermont museum teaches visitors about recycling.

RECYCLING REVOLUTION

Until recently, only about 35 percent of the waste produced in the state of Vermont was recycled or composted. In 2012, the state decided to change that.

The state government passed a law that made it illegal to throw away anything that could be recycled, such as cardboard, plastic bottles, garden waste, or food scraps. Many areas of the state also introduced "pay-as-you-throw" charges. People are charged based on how much trash they throw out.

Although it costs money to throw out waste in Vermont, recycling is free. This has made recycling a very popular choice.

SAVING WATER

In many places around the world, there is a shortage of water. It has become a precious resource. Eco-cities try to manage water responsibly, so that none is wasted.

GRAY WATER

One way of doing this is to recycle gray water. This is wastewater that comes from sinks, showers, and washing machines. It is fairly clean, because it doesn't include any wastewater from toilets.

Gray water can be treated and then reused for toilet flushing or watering gardens. Because the water is used twice, this is more eco-friendly than using clean water from a tap or hose.

WATER USE

Washing clothes
51 gallons
(193 liters)

In the United States, the average household uses 300 gallons (1,136 liters) of water per day.

Tap use
57 gallons
(216 liters)

Showering
60 gallons
(227 liters)

Toilet flushing
72 gallons
(273 liters)

These colorful containers collect rainwater for drinking.

RECYCLING WATER

Ivory Park is a poor area near the city of Johannesburg, South Africa. An organization called the EcoCity Trust has been working there to improve the residents' lives and make the city more eco-friendly. As a result of the Trust's work, many residents now have jobs growing food and collecting waste for the community.

Ivory Park also now recycles water. Some houses have systems to collect rainwater, so that it is not wasted. Gray water from homes is recycled for use in gardens. More than a dozen people have been trained in water recycling, and it is now their job to train their fellow residents.

GREEN SPACES

Eco-cities are designed so that humans and nature can coexist. Green spaces, such as parks and gardens, are an important part of an eco-city.

WHY GREEN SPACES MATTER

Trees and other plants absorb CO_2 from the air, which helps in the fight against **global warming**. The unpaved ground in green spaces also absorbs rainwater, which helps to avoid flooding. And parks provide somewhere for local wildlife to live.

Green spaces are also important for an eco-city's residents. Scientists have shown that when people have access to green spaces, they are more likely to be active. This helps to improve their health, which in turn makes people happier.

GREEN CITIES

Some cities have a lot more green space per person than others:

Tokyo, Japan
32.2 f² (3 m²)

London, U.K.
290.6 f² (27 m²)

Amsterdam, The Netherlands
489.75 f² (45.5 m²)

About five million people visit the High Line every year.

GARDEN IN THE SKY

The High Line was an elevated railway track that ran through New York City. For decades it was used by freight trains, but in 1980 it was abandoned. Local residents thought it would make a great park. It took a while, but in 2009 the first section was opened.

The High Line is now a corridor of green space that runs more than 1.24 miles (2 kilometers) through Manhattan. It is home to more than 200 types of plants, which have attracted birds, bees, and other wildlife. There are walking paths and sculptures for visitors to enjoy, too.

LOCAL FOOD

Eco-cities try to make use of local food, because most food is transported in vehicles that use fossil fuels. Food grown nearby doesn't have to travel so far, so less CO_2 is released.

THE CLOSER, THE BETTER

Big supermarket chains get their food from wherever they can buy it most cheaply. Sometimes, it even comes from another continent. In an eco-city, people are encouraged to support local food producers.

There may be small supermarkets that get food from nearby growers. Or residents can buy fruits, vegetables, flowers, and meat at farmers' markets. The food sold there is often fresher, as well as being more eco-friendly.

FOOD MILES

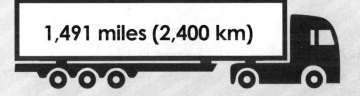

In the U.S.A., on average, food travels ...

1,491 miles (2,400 km)

... from farm to plate.

Non-local food transport creates up to ...

17 x as much CO_2

... as local food.

When food is transported long distances, a lot of carbon dioxide is released.

COMMUNITY GARDEN

In Berkhamsted, England, a local council and a charity have teamed up to start a community garden. It is part of an activity center that helps adults with learning disabilities develop new skills and train for jobs. They are taught how to take care of fruit trees and other plants.

The fruit and vegetables they grow are used to make meals for the workers—so it would be impossible for their meals to be any more local. Any leftover food is turned into jam, chutney, or juice, which is sold in the farm shop.

As an added bonus, members of the public are welcome to walk through the orchard and enjoy the relaxing green space.

City gardens give people who live in apartments the chance to grow their own food.

CITIES OF THE FUTURE

More than three billion people now live in cities, and the biggest cities have populations of more than 20 million people.

CHANGING OUR CITIES

It wouldn't be practical to abandon our existing cities and move to new eco-cities, built from scratch. Instead, cities need to constantly change and evolve. New buildings have to be more energy efficient. Public transportion needs to work well and use renewable energy.

Some of the world's greenest cities, such as Freiburg, Germany, are fairly small. But cities of every size, from small to giant, can make changes to reduce their impact on the planet. And in a giant city of 20 million people, even small changes can add up to make a big difference!

WORLD POPULATION

1980
4.4 billion

2015
7.3 billion

2050
9.5 billion
(predicted)

As the population increases, many more people will live in cities.

Treasure Island residents will get amazing views, along with eco-friendly living.

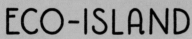

ECO-ISLAND

In 2011, San Francisco officials approved plans for a whole new eco-town to be built on two small islands in San Francisco Bay. They are Treasure Island, a former naval base, and neighboring Yerba Buena Island. The eco-town will have 8,000 homes, as well as hotels, restaurants, shops, and offices.

A ferry terminal will connect the eco-town to San Francisco, but residents will be able to get most of what they need without leaving. There will be green spaces, a school, and even an organic farm. Energy will be solar- and wind-powered. The town has been designed so that every home is within a 10-minute walk of all basic goods.

GLOSSARY

atmosphere A layer of gases that surrounds Earth

bacteria Tiny, single-celled organisms

carbon dioxide A gas produced by burning some types of fuel

carbon footprint The amount of carbon dioxide and other harmful gases released during an activity

climate change The gradual change in Earth's climate, brought about by global warming

compost To turn plant waste into fertilizer by letting it decay

emission Something that is released into the atmosphere, such as exhaust fumes from a car

fossil fuels Sources of energy, such as oil, coal, and natural gas, which are created from the long-dead remains of living things

global warming The gradual warming of Earth's temperature, caused partly by burning fossil fuels

insulation Building material used to stop a building heating up in summer and cooling down in winter

landfill A place where garbage is buried underground

natural resource Material from the natural world that can be used by people

power plant A facility that generates electricity

recycle To treat waste material so that it can be used again

renewable Able to be used without running out

solar panel A flat device that captures sunlight and turns it into electricity or uses it to heat water

thermal Energy in the form of heat

watt-hours A unit of power, usually electrical, equal to the energy produced by one watt in an hour

wind turbine A machine with rotating blades that turns wind into electricity

FINDING OUT MORE

WEBSITES

Play Go Green! to learn more about green transportation:
https://climatekids.nasa.gov/go-green/

Visit this website to learn which cities are the best at recycling waste:
https://kids.nationalgeographic.com/games/bb-quizzes/recycling-star-cities/

Explore a huge range of different types of eco-houses on this website:
www.ecofriendlyhouses.net

FURTHER READING

Leaving Our Mark, Reducing Our Carbon Footprint by Nancy Dickmann (Crabtree Publishing, 2016).

23 Ways to Be an Eco Hero by Isabel Thomas (QED Publishing, 2016).

How Community Gardens Work by Louise Spilsbury (Franklin Watts, 2015).

Living in a Sustainable Way, Green Communities by Megan Kopp (Crabtree, 2016).

How to Build a House by Isabel Thomas (Collins, 2016).

INDEX